Vehicle Service & Maintenance Log Book

Year: _____

Make: _____

Model: _____

Color: _____

Plate: _____

VIN: _____

Date	Mileage	Work Performed	Location	Cost

Date	Mileage	Work Performed	Location	Cost

Date	Mileage	Work Performed	Location	Cost

Date	Mileage	Work Performed	Location	Cost

Date	Mileage	Work Performed	Location	Cost

Date	Mileage	Work Performed	Location	Cost

Date	Mileage	Work Performed	Location	Cost

Date	Mileage	Work Performed	Location	Cost

Date	Mileage	Work Performed	Location	Cost

Date	Mileage	Work Performed	Location	Cost

Date	Mileage	Work Performed	Location	Cost

Date	Mileage	Work Performed	Location	Cost

Date	Mileage	Work Performed	Location	Cost

Date	Mileage	Work Performed	Location	Cost

Date	Mileage	Work Performed	Location	Cost

Date	Mileage	Work Performed	Location	Cost

Date	Mileage	Work Performed	Location	Cost

Date	Mileage	Work Performed	Location	Cost

Date	Mileage	Work Performed	Location	Cost

Date	Mileage	Work Performed	Location	Cost

Date	Mileage	Work Performed	Location	Cost

Date	Mileage	Work Performed	Location	Cost

Date	Mileage	Work Performed	Location	Cost

Date	Mileage	Work Performed	Location	Cost

Date	Mileage	Work Performed	Location	Cost

Date	Mileage	Work Performed	Location	Cost

Date	Mileage	Work Performed	Location	Cost

Date	Mileage	Work Performed	Location	Cost

Date	Mileage	Work Performed	Location	Cost

Date	Mileage	Work Performed	Location	Cost

Date	Mileage	Work Performed	Location	Cost

Date	Mileage	Work Performed	Location	Cost

Date	Mileage	Work Performed	Location	Cost

Date	Mileage	Work Performed	Location	Cost

Date	Mileage	Work Performed	Location	Cost

Date	Mileage	Work Performed	Location	Cost

Date	Mileage	Work Performed	Location	Cost

Date	Mileage	Work Performed	Location	Cost

Date	Mileage	Work Performed	Location	Cost

Date	Mileage	Work Performed	Location	Cost

Date	Mileage	Work Performed	Location	Cost

Date	Mileage	Work Performed	Location	Cost

Date	Mileage	Work Performed	Location	Cost

Date	Mileage	Work Performed	Location	Cost

Date	Mileage	Work Performed	Location	Cost

Date	Mileage	Work Performed	Location	Cost

Date	Mileage	Work Performed	Location	Cost

Date	Mileage	Work Performed	Location	Cost

Date	Mileage	Work Performed	Location	Cost

Date	Mileage	Work Performed	Location	Cost

Date	Mileage	Work Performed	Location	Cost

Date	Mileage	Work Performed	Location	Cost

Date	Mileage	Work Performed	Location	Cost

Date	Mileage	Work Performed	Location	Cost

Date	Mileage	Work Performed	Location	Cost

Date	Mileage	Work Performed	Location	Cost

Date	Mileage	Work Performed	Location	Cost

Date	Mileage	Work Performed	Location	Cost

Date	Mileage	Work Performed	Location	Cost

Date	Mileage	Work Performed	Location	Cost

Date	Mileage	Work Performed	Location	Cost

Date	Mileage	Work Performed	Location	Cost

Date	Mileage	Work Performed	Location	Cost

Date	Mileage	Work Performed	Location	Cost

Date	Mileage	Work Performed	Location	Cost

Date	Mileage	Work Performed	Location	Cost

Date	Mileage	Work Performed	Location	Cost

Date	Mileage	Work Performed	Location	Cost

Date	Mileage	Work Performed	Location	Cost

Date	Mileage	Work Performed	Location	Cost

Date	Mileage	Work Performed	Location	Cost

Date	Mileage	Work Performed	Location	Cost

Date	Mileage	Work Performed	Location	Cost

Date	Mileage	Work Performed	Location	Cost

Made in the USA
Middletown, DE
22 April 2022